God Will Not Close His Ears to Our Cry for Help

Caline B. Young

World rights reserved. This book or any portion thereof may not be copied or reproduced in any form or manner whatever, except as provided by law, without the written permission of the publisher, except by a reviewer who may quote brief passages in a review.

The author assumes full responsibility for the accuracy of all facts and quotations as cited in this book. The opinions expressed in this book are the author's personal views and interpretations, and do not necessarily reflect those of the publisher.

This book is provided with the understanding that the publisher is not engaged in giving spiritual, legal, medical, or other professional advice. If authoritative advice is needed, the reader should seek the counsel of a competent professional.

Cover Photo: Dmitrii/BigStock.com

Copyright © 2014 ASPECT Books
ISBN-13: 978-1-4796-0078-6 (Paperback)
ISBN-13: 978-1-4796-0079-3 (ePub)
ISBN-13: 978-1-4796-0080-9 (Mobi)
Library of Congress Control Number: 2013913563

Published by

*"I cried unto the Lord with my voice,
and he heard me out of his holy hill."
Psalm 3:4*

*"When he maketh inquisition for blood, he
remembereth them: he forgetteth not
the cry of the humble."
Psalm 9:12*

*"In my distress I called upon the Lord, and cried
unto my God: he heard my voice out of his temple,
and my cry came before him, even into his ears."
Psalm 18:6*

*"Our fathers trusted in thee: they trusted, and thou
didst deliver them. They cried unto thee, and
were delivered: they trusted in thee,
and were not confounded."
Psalm 22:4, 5*

*"Unto thee will I cry, O Lord my rock; be not silent
to me: lest, if thou be silent to me, I become like
them that go down into the pit. Hear the voice of
my supplications, when I cry unto thee, when I
lift up my hands toward thy holy oracle."
Psalm 28:1, 2*

*"I will extol thee, O Lord; for thou hast lifted me up,
and hast not made my foes to rejoice over me.
O Lord my God, I cried unto thee,
and thou hast healed me."
Psalm 30:1, 2*

*"I cried to thee, O Lord; and unto the Lord I made
supplication. What profit is there in my blood,
when I go down to the pit? Shall the dust praise
thee? Shall it declare thy truth? Hear, O Lord, and
have mercy upon me: Lord, be thou my helper.
Thou hast turned for me my mourning into
dancing: thou hast put off my sackcloth,
and girded me with gladness."
Psalm 30:8-11*

Table of Contents

Introduction 7
The Breath of Life is a Gift from God 9
Through Jesus We Keep the Good Faith 11
These Three are One 13
The Lord is Accompanying Me.........................15
Exceptional..17
I Was Lost One Day..19
Please Answer My Prayer 21
Death is Real 23
I Know He is Everywhere 25
You'll Fix Everything Just Right 27
"Blessed are the Poor in Spirit:
    for Theirs is the Kingdom of Heaven"..........29
Be Thankful...35
Jesus Saves..37
I Graduated 39
It's a Man's World 41
A Passing Grade 47
Lord, Let it Be for Me 51
Thanks 53
Walking and Praying..55
Pray to the Father in the Name of the Son........57

Why Didn't God Keep His Promise?...................59

I'll Obey in a Particular Way............................67

My Reward is with God 69

Ultimate Power and Support 71

I'm on God's Side..75

If I Don't Expand, I'll Ask for a Hand................77

A Warning to Help...79

I'll Have to Mind Me 81

Lord, Please Help Me 83

How Will I Know?..87

The Earth's Birthday Did Not Change 89

Sunlight 93

Fasting 95

God's Words are Important 97

Praying..101

Prayer is my Defense 103

Then Satan Will Leave Us..............................109

Introduction

Since my childhood I've always been jotting down poems, but I never took them seriously, until now. Now I'm hoping that people will gain a good insight of the true message that Jesus left.

Most of the time I say a prayer before I leave home to go somewhere. One day while on my way to see a sick person, I heard a voice say, "Medical attention." The voice was close to my ear. It was authoritative, but trusting that I would do the right thing. I heard the voice, but no one was present that I could see. Nevertheless, it was true. The person did need medical attention. From that day forward I knew that God had not given up on speaking to His children.

God is real. He hears us, and He will speak to us whenever He chooses. It is very important to pray and believe that our prayers will be answered. I thank the Lord for giving me wisdom.

The Breath of Life is a Gift from God

We have an excellent reason to be thankful to God every day, because we are using His breath to do our duty, which is to pray and ask God for help (James 1:5). Without oxygen (breath) as a life support, we would lie still, and we wouldn't have any knowledge or movement (Eccles. 12:7).

It is my opinion that God hears our every word. But to speak to Him directly in prayer would send part of His breath back to Him. It is a perfect way to contact God. Surely He recognizes untarnished words that we speak in His own breath (Job 27:3, 4).

Through Jesus We Keep the Good Faith

By the mighty power of God He can make
     the mountain rise (Matt. 19:26),
And the Ancient one of days can
     appear in the skies.
Intact He keeps it all;
His foundation does not fall.
He turns the blue sky into white across
     the mighty plains,
And all the colors remain the same
     without a naughty stain.
He is the greatest of the loyal.
He began us from the soil (Gen. 2:7).
He knows the will of every heart
And sees our thoughts before they
     start (Rom. 8:27).
I want to be in His command;
O by His grace I can.
We must focus on His grace,

And through Christ we keep the good faith (Eph. 2:8).

These Three are One

The Holy Ghost, the Father, and the
    Son—
They all are one (1 John 5:7).
They are and will forever be;
O let Them just remain in me.

The Son feels the rays of comfort that come from the Father (Luke 4:18), knowing that His Father is satisfied with Him gives Him strength. The heavenly Father delights in the Son's obedience (John 5:19-21) and gives Him a master-mind intelligence.

The Holy Ghost gives words to our mind if we are obedient to the Lord. The Holy Ghost comes within to give perfect movement to the whole body and to keep our whole being in comfort. It is

a perfect balance of content—a feeling where there is no complaint or discomfort (1 Cor. 6:19, 20).
The Holy Ghost, the Father, and the
    Son—
These three are one.
They are and will forever be.
O let Them just remain in me.

The Lord is Accompanying Me

O Lord, if I was perfect, I would solve
    the problems of women and men.
But I am not, so here I live within.
Within my body I decide where I'm
    going and what I want to do.
It is like living without the people
    around you.
I'm tired of living alone in this body of
    mine.
If You are there, Lord, please keep me
    in line.
I've wandered over so much ground,
But a friend within I have not found.
Stand back outside, troubles that focus
    on me.
Leave me on my own; let me be free.
The Lord is accompanying me,
Though it seems that I'm alone.

Look at the evidence—then it will be known.

Exceptional

A child had an assignment that had to be exceptional in order to pass to a higher grade at the end of the school year. I helped this child to make up a poem. The child read it to the class. The teacher sent the child to read it to the principal. The principal told the child to read it on the intercom so that everyone in the school could hear it being read. The child received good comments and did pass to the next grade. The poem was entitled, "I Was Lost One Day."

I Was Lost One Day

You'd believe that I'm sad to leave
    this place if you knew that at
    suppertime I say my grace.
I was lost one day; then the next day I
    found my way.
I was glad to come here, but my
    worries stopped my fear.
I did not care, because I made a plea,
    and my parents didn't hear.
I was lost one day; then the next day I
    found my way.
As the clock ticked away, I wasted my
    time.
Glad to awake soon enough to reach
    grade nine.
Please forgive me for being unkind.
God will leave the ninety-nine that are
    safe and come to find the one that

is lost (Matt. 18:12).
As a thousand years to God is only one
   day (2 Peter 3:8),
I'll still have time to find my way.

Please Answer My Prayer

The bright stars and the moon in the sky caused the night to be as light as a cloudy day. I knelt on the floor beside my bed and looked across the yard through my window as I began to pray.

I should have known then, as I know now, that the devil is at the root of every evil, bad, and sick situation. When my parents uttered loud, angry words and my father argued so fiercely, I was afraid that he might hurt my mother.

"Dear Lord," I prayed, "my father is angry at my mother. Please, God, don't let my father hurt my mother. If You will just let me know that my mother will be all right, I will lie down. I will go to sleep, and I will rest peacefully. Please, God, answer my prayer. Let me know somehow, in some way, that my mother will be OK."

After a short time of begging God to answer me, the Lord enlightened my eyes well enough for me to see a large wing sheltering the whole yard. It had not been there before, so I figured the Lord had caused me to see it. That, to me, was an answer to my prayer.

The sound of laughter awoke me at midnight. My mother and father were in the kitchen, the same place where they had argued. They were having a happy conversation.

Death is Real

(Genesis 5:5, 9:29; 23:2)

I never thought my mother would die, even though she was always telling me as I was growing up that everyone has to die.

I stood outside the examining room, unable to speak, after the doctor came out and told me that they could not cure my mother. I cried—yes, I cried a lot. I could not believe that my mother would die. Every opportunity I had alone, I prayed for my mother's recovery. When I prayed, I visualized her drifting slowly toward the ground. I wouldn't face the fact that she was dying, even after seeing indications to prove it. I thought that I was being ignored by the Supreme Being. So I kept praying and thinking that I would get the attention I desired.

I was in so much pain when my

mother breathed her last breath. In order to snap out of it enough to prevent myself from having a heart attack, I decided to keep a promise I had made to her as I bandaged her stomach after surgery. I joined an agency so I could be sent to help people who lived in their homes but were too sick to do all they needed to do for themselves. God has aided me many times while I strove to do this kind of work.

I Know He is Everywhere

(John 14:16-18)

When I'm outside among the trees,
I believe that God is in the breeze.
He is in the flowers and the air;
I know that He is everywhere.
Inside the house He is not away from me,
Also outside He will be.
I need God to comfort me when I am sad,
I need Him to say that I'm not bad,
That the way I feel is all wrong,
And soon He will make me forever strong.
O Lord, You know where I am and what I'm doing.
You are keeping me afloat
Without me letting You know by note.
Thank You, God; wherever I go You are there.

I am aware of Your presence everywhere!

You'll Fix Everything Just Right

Lord, it's OK; You're in charge.
We want to do whatever You expect of us.
But don't let evil block the view—
We want to keep in touch with You.
You sent Your Son to die for us in
    order that we may be freed of sin.
You taught us that You exist.
You gave us the opportunity to trust in
    You.
Lord, it's OK; You're in charge.
I know where You were when I was in
    pain:
You were preparing a place for me,
    so that wherever You are, I will be
    (John 14:2, 3).
Lord, it's OK; You're in charge.
Judge me and please find me innocent.
Please try me and find me fair

(Ps. 139:23, 24).

Please let me see and know that You are here.

Lord, it's OK; You're in charge.

When I rise, please put on me immortality.

I will accept Your measure and all pleasure.

You'll fix everything just right.

My heart will be at peace whether it's day or night.

"Blessed are the Poor in Spirit: for Theirs is the Kingdom of Heaven"

(Matt. 5:3, KJV)

I always like to save that which appears to be OK. To save everything that I think is OK would bring a pile of stuff into my home that most people would consider junk. It would clutter up my house. This I learned by doing. If I ordered something from the store, and the container that held it was firm, I kept the container for a while until I had to force myself to throw it away. When food went bad, I worried that I had left it around too long before eating it. But something is going to go bad sometime. So I have to convince myself it's OK; that's normal. I have this way about me to save, save, save. But I can be reasonable about it.

Once someone gave me a coat that was too large for me. I decided I was not going to put them through the trouble of exchanging it. I kept it, hoping I would meet a person that it would fit. Then I would give it away.

I really did like that coat. So I made up my mind that as soon as I gave it away, I would buy a similar coat. It would be the same leopard print, but instead of being three-quarter length, it would reach my knees.

The day came when I met a girl whom it did fit, and she was very much in need of a coat. So I gave my coat to her. Then I went to search for the same type of coat. I went to the store where the coat had been purchased. It was not there. I traveled to many stores. A leopard-print coat could not be found. I was facing an impossible situation (Matt. 19:26).

I became tired, so I called on God. "Lord, You know where that coat is. So many times You have helped me. I know

You can do it this time. I tried very hard to get the coat that I like. I can't find it. I don't know where it could be. I'm pleading with You to tell me. Please! I really want a coat like the one I gave away. And You know where I can go to get it. Please help me to find it."

Just then I saw words in the atmosphere, close to my eyes. "LORD & TAYLOR" were the words. The Lord & Taylor store was a long way from where I lived. Promptly I put my $200 in my pocket and started out for the store. After one hour of traveling, I arrived and went inside to the coat department. I saw my coat as I was about to go in. It was hanging in clear view among the other coats. I saw on the tag that the price was $400. But it was on sale for $200! "Thank You, God," I said with much gratitude.

We should not rely upon others to get an answer from God for us. The only way we can resist a lot of wrongdoing is to have God take control in our lives. Because the devil is stronger than we are, we must be devoted to the commandments of God and the words of Jesus Christ.

While I was praying, "O God, please lead me and guide me so that I can follow," I had no ability to follow unless God sent the devil away. The devil will leave by faith and prayer to the Lord. The power of evil can stifle our will to resist. It is praying and believing in God that moves us out of the darkness.

When one of my brothers died, a lady prayed for me solemnly. She said to God over and over, "Lord, please comfort Caline." When she was finished praying, God gave me a vision of myself entering the hospital while my brother was alive and going down the corridor. I saw my brother sick in bed behind a glass wall. Peace entered me and surrounded me perfectly. I knew that God loved him and that there is safety when we have confidence in God. We must pray for ourselves and others whenever we can so that the devil cannot find a way into our hearts and minds to cause weakness in order to turn us away from God.

There is power in a group that is praying. There is a comfort and support that resonates from one to another. Now that my earthly father has died, I miss the connection that I had with him and the support that I felt from his love.

Jesus said, "For where two or three are gathered together in my name, there am I in the midst of them" (Matt. 18:20, KJV). There is power in contacting God in prayer. The Lord saves us when we trust in Him through prayer. His answer will come in a way that is right for us.

Be Thankful

Once when my parents had to take care of an errand, they left me in charge. So I gave lunch to my three brothers. I served each one of us a bowl of soup, a glass of water, and one biscuit. After we sat down, I began to say grace. My brothers laughed at me, because no food was left. I had given them such a small bowl that they had already eaten it all! They teased me for not having more to give them. Also, I had no dessert, so they wondered what we had to be thankful for.

We were sitting at the table, which was by the window. When I turned my head to look out the window, I saw words. The words were not on paper. They were not on the window. The words were not on the ground, either. They were outside the window in *midair*. Each letter in each word had the colors of a rainbow—red, yellow, orange, green, and purple. "PROPHESY UNTO

THEM," the capital letters stated. What they meant, I didn't know. My brothers never knew that I saw those words. They disappeared after I had read them.

As years passed, I became aware of what those words meant. This is what I said to my brothers while I was thinking about those words: "Even if you have a glass of water when you are hungry, it is something to be thankful for. All belongs to God. Being thankful for small things is a way of being content with God, which is a prayer of faith that blesses you with bigger and better glory from the Lord (Matt. 6:31-33). God hears prayers, and He also fulfills our needs."

Jesus Saves

One way a person is blessed by reading the whole Bible from Genesis to Revelation is that his or her wisdom in understanding God increases. Jesus saves by the power of the Holy Spirit. Reading the Bible helps us to understand what God expects of us.

Sacrificing lambs to take away people's sins and the act of atonement that cleansed the temple once a year were all in the past long before my father was born. But he had a point when he said, "No one should accept a church where the priest sits in a confession area to hear the sins of the congregation as each person talks to him privately. The priest cannot forgive sin. The people should pray to God directly for the forgiveness of sins. No man on earth has the power to forgive sins."

It is written that Jesus took the place of the sacrifice when He died on the cross. It is written that Jesus is "the Lamb of God, which taketh away the sin of the world" (John 1:29, KJV).

Our closeness to God through prayer, our continued accountability for our sins, and the forgiveness of our sins through repentance determine our destination at the end of this world.

I Graduated

As far back as when I was thirteen years old, I always believed that God could save me from whatever problem I had or would have. This is the reason I pressed on and stayed in school at fifty years old, even when the teacher told me to start over after I had studied for a month.

When I entered the building to go up the five steps that lead to the elevator, I was confident, although I had seen dark shadows climbing the same stairway in a vision. I wrote a speech entitled "It's a Man's World" (see next chapter) to display my true feelings after I had graduated.

I had a difficult time with my typing speed. I went to school off and on for three months after graduation time to be sure I could type more than forty words a minute. I received awards, my diploma, and excellent grades.

It's a Man's World

After attending school at General Communications for a while I became aware of the fact that it is a man's world.

We have excellent teachers at General Communications. But it has always been clear to me that from the beginning would be a perfect way to start teaching a subject. To begin in the middle or the end or even to skip here and there would prevent us from grasping the subject or linking the whole in order.

The first night I attended this school, Mrs. Weith announced in the typing class that everyone has to type forty words a minute in order to pass. I realize now that this was the end; without accomplishing this I wouldn't be able to finish the course.

During the second period Mrs. Drilliah told the class to start in the middle of the book. I searched the front part of the book and realized that as high school graduates we were expected to know the beginning before we arrived.

When the first month ended, I was told by Mrs. Debau, the computer teacher, that I should take her class over. I was upset. "How do you feel about this?" she asked. I didn't answer her. I walked away from her down the hallway where she had spoken to me.

I went home without attending all my classes that night. On my way home I thought, *As a child I went from the first grade to the twelfth. I missed many days of school each year, but I did not repeat a grade—not even once! But at General Communications I've been in class whenever I was expected to be there. Then why is this happening? Why is she doing this to me?*

The Lord said that I could come to

this school! I remembered. With this thought I pondered my situation. *First, there is a tremendous strain on me. I've never had to go to school and work on the same day every day. I'm tired at times, which means that I can't always concentrate fully on what I'm doing. Also, before I started this class, I had never in my whole life touched a computer or known anything about the way a computer works. Mrs. Debau started teaching from the beginning of the book. She wanted me to know exactly how to boot up and how to save my document. I don't know why I thought I could catch up somewhere along the way.*

I was exhausted. Like a child that is crying because she needs a nap, I wiped the tears from my eyes continuously all the way home. I convinced myself that I could do whatever should be done, because the Lord had said I could come to this school (Phil. 4:13).

With Jesus as my first friend, at the top of my list, I returned to school the first night of the second module. Mrs. Debau exclaimed, "You came back!" I didn't say anything. In later days I learned that since Mrs. Debau is the director of General Communications, she has the authority to dismiss people or keep them aboard. She has a difficult job to do. I sympathize with her.

Once Robert, one of the class members, said to me, "There's Caline with that confident look." He said this without knowing that my confidence was founded on something God had said: "And this is the confidence that we have in him, that, if we ask any thing according to his will, he heareth us" (1 John 5:14, KJV).

I received a Positive Mental Award from Mrs. Drilliah. To me Mrs. Weith's attitude was "Whatever will be will be," and I appreciated that very much.

In my opinion Mr. Atefpro is a very good teacher. He stays on a subject until he is absolutely sure he has given all that he can give.

Mrs. Drilliah is a cheerful person. Raise your hand in her class and you are allowed to answer. A word of warning: Raise your hand in Mr. Atefpro's English class only for exercise, because you will get tired enough to put it down. He would rather call on someone who does not know the answer. Isn't that very domineering? He may be domineering, but this world does not belong to men. It belongs to God (Gen. 2:4).

Jesus came to die for us (John 1:29). He is the one who gave me confidence. He said I could attend this school! I can accomplish anything if I'm not going against His will (Phil. 4:13).

A Passing Grade

When I was a girl, my father talked about the cruel way in which white slave owners treated their black slaves before the Civil War was won. He even told some of the bad things that were done so that black slaves would remain loyal to their masters.

I'm thankful for the accomplishments made by the black people for equality. I'm also thankful to Jesus for dying on the cross to save all nations from the unjust way that comes from the source of evil (John 3:16; Galatians 6:14-18).

Through prayer God will support us in solving our problems and will aid us in our needs.

Integration: a get-together thing;
Segregation: apart we sing.
Down upon the years from whence we came,
Our race endured so much shame
By being tortured as slaves.
Many met with their graves.
It seemed that blacks were different than whites,
That our path foreshadowed the light.
God did not say we're the worst (1.Sam. 16:7).
But prejudice condemned us like a curse.
Committees did discuss the matter.
Faithful blacks cried unto God for the latter.
One man said, "No violence."
His name was Martin King, and king I consider him to be,
Even if someone may threaten me.
By those that stood up for us,
There became a law as thus:
God's commandments helped us to stand (John 15:10, 11).

We'll always have a right to demand.
God is against prejudiced actions.
He approves the right reactions.
By God we've gotten far ahead.
From God we received a passing grade
   (Rev. 5:9).

Lord, Let it Be for Me

You've heard the saying, Whatever will be will be.
But you can say, "Lord, let it be for me."
A promise from God is a dream come true;
While failing you can rise to start anew.
So don't tarry because of the heavy load;
Carry on; follow the code.
In this world there is enough for you;
God wants your good dreams to come true.
You've heard the saying, Whatever will be will be.
But you can say, "Lord, let it be for me."

As we began we did abide with Him;
Before conception we're smaller than a stem.
Look at yourself and see what God has made.
He is with you; do not be afraid.
He'll go with you, never mind your whim,
Even if the light is growing dim.
You've heard the saying, Whatever will be will be.
But you can say, "Lord, let it be for me."
Think of whom you have to count on.
Retain your hope; you are not alone.
Strive for the good of each day.
Keep the faith and a merry way.
It is better to count on a promise going through,
Than to think God has forgotten you.
You've heard the saying, Whatever will be will be.
But you can say, "Lord, let it be for me."

Thanks

Lord, please give us Your hand
As Your Spirit aids us in our plan.
Lord, I'll be reaching out to You
In everything I undertake to do.
I know You are near.
All my prayers You will hear.
All that is gone and has been
We realize You did send;
Nothing on this earth came from man,
Even if it was made by hands.
From You no one can take,
Which is why You gave the knowledge to make.
So we will kneel and give thanks to You,
Because this is what You expect us to do.

Walking and Praying

I was praying as I was walking home from work. I had to walk ten blocks, and there was a store called Zayres in about the third block from where I lived.

I wanted an inexpensive dress to wear to an important occasion. I didn't know where to go to buy something that would please me. So I prayed and prayed. "Where should I go, Lord? You know the best place. Please tell me so I don't have to search for a long time—even for days. The time is at hand, Lord. I do not have many days. I need the dress now. Please, Lord, tell me where it is. You know everything. You are able to help me. Please help me!"

The word "Zayres" appeared close to my eyes. "Oh," I whispered. "The Lord answered me! What a miracle! Thank You, Lord. Who would believe this if I told them?" I was so delighted and glad that I was talking out loud, even though no one was around to hear the good news.

I went inside Zayres and found a low-priced dress. It looked presentable enough to wear to the wedding.

Because God knows all and can do all, He answered my prayer. He did say, "Ask, and ye shall receive" (John 16:24, KJV). And I did believe with all my heart that He would answer me (Matt. 9:28, 29).

Pray to the Father in the Name of the Son

(John 5:22, 23)

It was in the month of October when I jaywalked to quickly find shelter from the cold wind. A man was driving toward me at a safe distance from me. When he came near where I stood at the bus stop, he yelled with all his strength, "You jaywalking idiot!" I was not in his path, but that is the way Satan works. He causes others to help him in an unkind way. This time I was very thankful that I sensed protection, a security that prevented him from physically harming me.

The Comforter (the Holy Spirit) will give a person a sense of peace, no matter what danger lurks in the way. The Comforter comes from the Lord (John 16:7). We can invite the Lord to come into our heart when we go by the teaching of the Bible. We must make up our minds to do our best to keep the commandments of God, to have the spirit of prophecy (the testimony of Jesus Christ), and to get baptized by immersion.

We must not give up after baptism. We need the Comforter always so we will be guided and taught by the Holy Spirit (John 14:26). This will help to set us free from the power of evil.

Once the Lord Jesus stood in front of me. I felt a spray falling on me. I believe sincerely that it was a force of the Comforter. It was when I was being troubled by a serious matter. I was praying desperately. He made me feel worry-free. I felt as though it would be OK. What I thought was a problem was no longer anything to worry about.

All authority has been given to Jesus, the Son of God, because He paid the price for the forgiveness of sins (Matt. 28:18). Now we must pray to the Father in the name of the Son (John 16:23).

Why Didn't God Keep His Promise?

In Sligo Sabbath school class on February 4, 1995, my granddaughter's birthday was celebrated. We stopped in the public library on our way home. I showed her a memory verse in the quarterly. "The Lord watches over all who love Him, and Jesus loves all the children in the world," I told her.

She pointed to a drawing and said, "That's Jesus. Which one is God, Grandma?"

"We call Jesus the Son of God. Jesus and God live in heaven. When we pray, we call upon the Father in the name of the Son, and by the Holy Spirit we receive help (John 14:16, 17; John 15:26).

I started to think of the miracles that God had performed in my life. I remembered a Sunday night when I was on my way to work. There was a fear inside me that started as soon as I stepped off the bus to walk down a dark road.

Just the night before I had been explaining to a woman about the perfect way to get around Satan's tricks and schemes. He really is able to be a demon inside a person, but the Spirit of God is able to push him out. Praying to God causes him to run away (1 Peter 5:6, 8, 10, 11). So now I was worried that the devil would try to get even with me this very night.

"God, I have walked on a dark road before, but tonight it is different. Satan wants to hurt me. Please, God, stay with me this night, and I will be safe," I prayed. There were many cars going up and down Montgomery Avenue, but I loved to go to my patient's house. It was so peaceful there.

As I walked, I kept in mind that I must change my schedule to Monday nights. On Sunday nights I had to walk a mile to work from the bus stop. On Monday nights the bus would take me all the way to work.

I came to an intersection, where a car was ready to go onto the main road when its turn came up. I was passing in front of it after it came to a full stop. The car slowly moved toward me, which caused me to get out of its path in a hurry. The young man who was driving let out a loud laugh.

I would have gotten his tag number, but it was too dark for me to see it. So I hurried on and prayed, "Please, Lord, I beg of You to send the good angel to watch over me. I need to be safe from the devil's intentions."

When I was inside my patient's home that night, the Spirit of God reached out to me. Inside my head it was as if it was a dream, but I was fully awake. I saw a white cloud coming from my home on the road I had traveled, instilling peace and power within me. Even though it did not talk, the Spirit instilled a knowledge in me to know the Spirit of God by instinct as it entered my body from miles away. (I was at least 36 miles from home.)

Just before the white cloud disappeared from my sight, the Lord laid a promise in my heart and mind. He promised He would be with me on my way to work. I wondered why He did not promise that He would be with me on my way home, too. I concluded that maybe some terrible thing was to take place on my way to work, not on my way home.

The second day after the promise, before 6:00 a.m. I was on my way to work, walking down a steep hill and thinking I must be careful on the wet grass. Still, I started to run. I slipped, falling forward on my face and hitting a rock. When I got up and felt my face, I decided I had not broken my jawbone. But blood was coming from my eye. The metro station was near me, so I thought I would clean myself in the bathroom there and be OK to go to my workplace.

When I looked in the mirror, I became depressed, as there was an open wound under the bottom lashes of my eye. I tried not to cry, for fear that the bleeding would become worse. The exterior of my whole eye was black and blue by this time, and the redness inside my eye looked like a thick layer of blood. The front of my coat was covered with dirt, which I had not noticed before, and the knees of my pants had dirt and grass stains on them. Through all this I hadn't felt any pain.

I went immediately to the hospital, where the doctor stitched the wound and covered my eye with a patch. The doctor and the nurse were very nice to me. When the doctor entered the room, he introduced himself as Doctor Bentman. The nurse held on to me while encouraging me to be perfectly still while Doctor Bentman closed up the gash. Before Doctor Bentman left the room, he made me laugh by saying;

"If you can't remember my name, think of a bent man."

After 24 hours the ophthalmologist took the patch off and gave me medicine for pain. Even though I was not in pain, I feared I would be, so I took one pain pill after leaving the ophthalmologist's office. After taking the pain pill, I felt dizzy and nauseous. I drank a large glass of cold water, and the sickness slowly went away.

After four days the stitches were removed. My entire eye was black and blue, and the inside was as red as it could be.

Through the whole episode, I wondered, Where was God when I got hurt? Why didn't God keep His promise? There was only one rock in the area where I fell. It was as if fate had brought me to it, and it was beyond my control to change the unexpected.

On my last visit to the doctor, he said my eye would be all right. He also said, "Be careful. One lady came in here not long ago. She had severed her eye."

It was only then that I realized that God *had* kept His promise! It was through my own carelessness that I had gotten hurt. But I hadn't sustained any permanent damage. After fourteen days the redness was gone; both eyes looked the same. I was all right! Thanks be to God!

I'll Obey in a Particular Way

They say You live in heaven above,
But on earth You show great love.
Lord, I'm aware of what they say,
And I'll obey in a particular way.
We must honor the straight and
 narrow way.
The wide way carries on whatever way
 every day (Matt. 7:13).
They say many have their reward;
The straight must wait to sit with God
 (Matt. 7:14).
Lord, I'm aware of what they say,
And I'll obey in a particular way.
Your Son died to pay alms for me.
Still I'm not free.
They say the Father is about;
We must trust in Him without a doubt.
Lord, I'm aware of what they say,

And I'll obey in a particular way.
We cannot do right alone;
We must pray God's name in each tone.
They say in God we must believe
To obtain salvation when we leave.
Lord, I'm aware of what they say,
And I'll obey in a particular way.
The Lord will fill that space within.
It's called lonely we have been.
They say God will watch over us.
This settlement of God is just.
Lord, I'm aware of what they say,
And I'll obey in a particular way.

My Reward is with God

The devil is a fraud. Can he take away
  my reward?
He can take away my reward, if I live
  by his fib.
The truth is in the Bible.
Hit the right cord;
My reward is with God.
Sinning will lead me to die with the
  devil. All bad comes from him.
He does not have a good place to stay.
He leads us in a gloom of gray.
My reward is with God.
If I burn in hellfire, how will I get my
  reward?
The devil wants to lead me to the
  flames. I will escape.
My reward is with God.
I'll read and see how good I can be.

The Bible has a truth
In the eighth book of Ruth.
There is lying and cheating in Satan's rules.
To God we pray without tools.
My reward is with God!

Ultimate Power and Support

Through kindness and the power of God, we reach out to each other. This is something that proves we all need each other (Eph. 4:25).

The power of God is written in the gospel of Mark (Mark 5:25-34). In the crowd was a woman who had been suffering from chronic bleeding for 12 years. She came from behind Jesus in the crowd and touched the hem of Jesus' garment.

"Who touched my clothes?" Jesus asked. He had felt a part of His power to heal go out of Him, because she was healed after touching His garment.

When a sick person is delighted to have the company of another, that delight gives the other person a boost. The people I helped—the people who had strokes, heart conditions, and breathing problems—gave me a reward. I could feel their support. It welled up inside me like overflowing energy. It kept me going long after quitting time. My patients lifted my spirits, and I in turn hoped to lift their spirits.

I was fueled by the thought that the patients who looked forward to my return. Their gratitude kept me going and helped me to pour my energies into comforting them and taking care of them. Without saying a word, they reached out to me through their smiles and body language. Like a light that spots an object, and, if it is strong enough, creates heat, these unseen rays of thankfulness alerted me to the fact that they were glad to have me around.

Being happy and giving praise helps a person to feel that all is well with them. It brings peace of mind with energy to spare for many tasks. When we communicate in a kind voice and have a soft expression in our eyes, we are having compassion for another (Mark 8:2).

When someone is angry at us, it produces negative thoughts and feelings. Through prayer God can remove those negative feelings and restore our self-worth, knowing that we are His children.

We can be at peace with our enemies and retain a positive spirit by the help of God through prayer. We cannot lean on God if we harbor anger toward those who hurt us. If we hold sincerely to the belief that God hears and will answer us, we will be blessed by His power—a power that solves all problems.

I'm on God's Side

Not just anything will do for me.
I'm on God's side, you see.
Going up and down, right or wrong, is
    not the way I go.
Not just anything will do for me.
Some things are better than others. I
    won't do everything.
I'll just carry the right melody.
I'll carry the tradition of God,
And I'll fetch the right reward.
Everything seems to be perfect when
    we get on top.
Be sure the package doesn't drop.
Can we say the message of the Bible is
    right? It says not just anything will
    do.
It says make the right move. And what
    does the right move include?

It says God is first.
Anything else is worse,
Because God made me and He made
 you—
Tell me this is something you can do.
If you can't, you are worse and God is
 first.
Not just anything will do for me.
I'm on God's side, you see!

If I Don't Expand, I'll Ask for a Hand

I know subtraction; now I need satisfaction.
You said, "Don't be late." What about fate?
I may swerve and run over a curb.
Leave me alone; I'll come home.
You think you know when you don't see, so deep down you interfere with me.
My IQ is getting better all the time, and physically I'm fine.
I know I must strive for a gold. I don't need to be told.
I'm a growing young man. Please understand!
You think you know when you don't see, so deep down you interfere with me.

My friends are all right; they don't keep
  me out at night.
As another person I grew; I'm not the
  same as you.
You think you know when you don't
  see, so deep down you interfere
  with me.
Before you ask if my lights blink, give
  me time to think.
God is my friend; He always has been.
If I don't expand, I'll ask for a hand!

A Warning to Help

I have noticed that if I hear someone calling my name, and that person is not within calling distance, it is a vision. It is the Spirit of the Lord sending that person's voice so I will know to help them when they ask. Or if they don't ask and I can see that I should come to their aid, then I should help them.

If there is a voice telling me to hurt someone, I will not do as that voice says. The evil one's voice leads people in such a way. The Lord would not tell me to hurt anyone. "Vengeance is mine; I will repay," says the Lord (Romans 12:19, KJV). Defending myself is different, but God will not accept hurting a person just to do something (Rev. 12:7-9).

If we read the whole Bible, we will

get a perfect understanding of what is right with God and what is not.

I'll Have to Mind Me

In the mirror I see that I am tall,
But my actions make me look small.
Sit down, Mother; give me some time.
I need someone to mind.
You said Jesus loves a child.
Will Jesus talk to me a while?
If you only work,
How can I know where Jesus lurked?
When I read, I want to summarize,
But my decisions are not wise.
Take a vacation. You must!
We have some things to discuss.
You said Jesus loves a child.
Will Jesus talk to me a while?
Wherever Jesus lurks, can I find Him?
You said I could talk to Him, even
    when the light is dim.
You said in the Bible His words will be.

The words of Jesus I must see,
Or I'll have to mind me.

Lord, Please Help Me

(Matt. 6:13; 2 Peter 2:9)

The light is dim along the way;
Lord, please help me to see the day.
I know the devil has power over me;
Save me, Lord; You must agree.
I made a choice.
Please hear my voice.
Of all on earth,
I take You first.
I will not pray before images.
Let them all be smitten down,
Even if I kneel upon the ground.
The light is dim along the way;
Lord, please help me to see the day.
Don't let the spirit of Satan enter my
    mind.
Help me to leave him far behind.
I will not take Your name in vain.
I will not use it unless I praise or pray.
I will be calling on You day by day.

The devil hurries to get between,
But I want my body to be clean.
The light is dim along the way;
Lord, please help me to see the day.
As I grew and grew, I slowly learned of
    You.
Now I know You rested on Saturday.
Saturday is the birthday of the earth.
What a calm day it must have been;
I'd like to have been there then
    (Exod. 20:10; Matt. 12:8; Mark
    1:21; James 2:10).
The light is dim along the way;
Lord, please help me to see the day.
My parents meant a lot to me,
Though sometimes we did disagree.
Now that You took them away,
Let them live in Your kingdom, I pray.
Lord, I have been mean;
Of my sins You have seen.
From the dragon that dwells in me,
Please, Lord, set me free.
The light is dim along the way;
Lord, please help me to see the day.
My husband is my only bind.

Why is there another function in line?
Lord, if You stand close to me,
The serpent cannot get around Thee.
He takes control of my mind,
Even when I don't drink wine.
Sometimes he stands in the center of
    Your temple;
Lord, where are You?
I can't stop him. What will I do?
The light is dim along the way;
Lord, please help me to see the day.
O God, just sit within my heart,
And tell Satan he will not.
Then I cannot do Satan's will.
I will not covet, steal, or kill;
My mind will be pure and clear.
The dragon I will not fear.
Where I live is not a good place to be.
The serpent has an advantage over me.
The light is dim along the way;
Lord, please help me to see the day.

How Will I Know?

I planted a tree. How will I know
That God made it grow?
Because when I say, "Grow!"
The tree does not know.
Is God in the wind?
If He won't answer, how will I know?
Because only God can cause the wind
 to blow.
During the earthquake, how do we
 know that God moved the ground
 out of its place?
We cannot strive with His pace.
Is God in my body?
If He does not answer me, how will I
 know?
Because I can't survive when my
 breath goes (Gen. 2:7).

The Earth's Birthday Did Not Change

I sat there and saw the leaves shimmer in the sunlight as one by one they swirled from the trees. And I thought, *How beautiful the world is from where I sit, with everything falling into place as each thing takes a turn to be born.* The seeds from the limbs bring forth trees, and the trees are born. The trees are covered by the leaves growing on the limbs, so that I can't see in the wooded area. The leaves turn from green to red, yellow, purple, and brown. They fall from the trees and leave so many empty limbs. Then I'm not blocked from seeing in the wooded area.

With so many changes being brought about by God as He develops things, it is great that God remains steadfast to His

Word. If He says, "Thou shalt have no other gods before me" (Exod. 20:3), He means what He says. If He says, "Thou shalt not make unto thee any graven image" (Exod. 20:4), He means what He says. If He says, "Thou shalt not take the name of the Lord thy God in vain" (Exod. 20:7), He means what He says. He will not change.

Also He said, "Remember the sabbath day, to keep it holy" (Exod. 20:8). Then why do some take Sunday as the Sabbath day? If they rest and are peaceful on Sunday, will God change and say Saturday is not the Sabbath day?

God took six days to make the earth. God rested on the seventh day because the earth had been born. It is similar to a mother waiting for her baby to be born. She has to wait nine months for the baby to develop, and that will be the set time for birth. The birthday cannot be changed—just like the birthday of the earth. It cannot be changed. There was a set time for the earth to be born.

The earth does harbor bad people and people who try very hard to be good. But God will not change His commandments (Matt. 5:18).

Sunlight

Wouldn't it be great if we were so righteous that our image was as bright as the sun?

The Lord sends forth His light—the one that rises in the east. God made it a clear image. And it continues to stand, even though this could be a tiresome task. Its smile is in the way God made it shine.

People look toward the east, the north, the south, and the west. If they do not see the sun, they wonder if a storm is beginning—a hurricane or a tornado—or if it's just going to rain.

This is one way God carries on His work. His goodness comes through the sun.

The devil smothers our good intentions. We would like to have a glow like the sun in us. God's sunlight shows how it can be within a soul (John 3:20, 21; John 12:35, 36).

We need to do right in order to prevail. We will pray that by the grace of God, His permanent light will continue to shine through us.

Fasting

If we are fasting, it is a cry for help. When Jesus was fasting, it was a way to prove Himself. It was a way to prove that He would continue on the intended path, no matter how eagerly Satan tried to push his way in and interrupt Jesus' intentions.

With fasting we desperately reach out to God in prayer for whatever reason is behind our fasting. We neglect ourselves to claim a desperate need. And God will answer us in a way that is best for us. God gave Jesus strength enough to take on the punishment that He went through. Jesus paid the price for our sins. The Lord knows our problems before we ask for help. Fasting and praying reveals our dependence upon

God (Mark 9:29).

Fasting helps us to maintain our undying faith. Our burdens will be lifted, and we will be able to carry on in a better way (Matt. 11:28).

But to ask is exercising freedom of choice. It is a way of being aware that God will not force us to serve Him. And we feel content with ourselves when there is freedom of choice about anything, especially to choose and pray to the One who created us. He knows our problems before we ask for anything (Matt. 6:5, 6). Fasting is a good way to get problems solved that we can't solve ourselves.

God's Words are Important

Jesus left His teachings in the Bible. We cannot get to heaven if we don't care about the will of God. We must be motivated to do the will of God. We must keep in touch with the words of God. When Jesus came, He tried very much to help us understand how God the Father wants us to serve Him. Jesus prayed, and He asked God the Father to take away the suffering that He had to go through, but He was willing to suffer if that was the only way to pay the price to save us from Satan (Matt. 26:39–42).

We are so gullible that we easily sin. If we read over Jesus' teachings in the Bible, time after time, as often as possible, we will begin to understand everything. It is a way to keep in mind as to how to serve God. We must follow the exact instructions that are left in the bible about whatever Jesus taught. The things that Jesus taught before He died have been written in the New Testament of the Bible.

One of the chapters in the New Testament that is easy to understand is Romans chapter 8.

Because Jesus died to get rid of our sins, we must be put under the water during baptism in order to leave our sins behind. It is a symbolism of dying to self and being buried in the water and raised to a new life in Christ.

Jesus died and pardoned us from our sins, and He will come back to us. We show that we are getting rid of our sins the same as Jesus did, which is a way to prove that we appreciate all that Jesus went through to save us. Through baptism, we show that we are doing the best we can to get away from the devil's influence.

God will help us. God will not close His ears to our cry for help (1 Peter 5:7)!

Praying

We must pray when we feel that there is no need to pray, because someone else needs our prayers. Your prayer will help to stop whatever is holding people back from knowing the will of God.

We must pray when we are sick or if there is an undertaking that we desire to be successful (Matt. 21:22).

We must pray even when the future looks very bright, and it would seem that nothing could go wrong. We don't want the devil to find a way to make us sad. We know that the enemy (Satan) wants to stop us so that we will not serve God. Serving God is doing whatever

Jesus taught us to do. The Bible teaches us the right way to obey God.

If we pray and ask God to help us to obey Him, He will help us because we are His children (Matt. 6:7–9), Pray so that you can be helped and influenced by God. Pray to stay strong enough to resist temptation.

The devil is stronger than us. We know that we can't rise in defense against an invisible being. Through prayer, God will help us to be safe from the devil. God is able to do what has to be done to stop the devil, whenever it is God's will.

Prayer is my Defense

When Brenda chose to travel the abandoned railroad she immediately prayed, "God, I know You exist, and I can depend on You to keep me safe." She recalled the words her grandfather had spoken as he stood in the doorway when she left his house. "I will say a long prayer for you, so that God will guide you safely. Don't forget to phone me when you get to your house." The words her brother had spoken to her many times, also could not be excluded from her brain. "Don't walk on the railroad," he had said. "Racist people linger among the trees. They are dope addicts. When they are high on marijuana, they react to their prejudice minds stronger than when they are not intoxicated."

Brenda could have walked along the highway, but people often stopped to tell her that she should drive a car. And if someone did offer her a ride and she didn't accept, they would waste her time trying to pry the reason out of her. Not being in the mood to listen to their persuasions, she started to walk along the dark charcoal stones and on the large boards that steady the railing on each side of the railroad, which was the only way to avoid their interference. It sort of quieted her fear when she repeated the words, "God knows, God cares," and remembered her grandfather was praying for her.

Brenda was thinking that God did say that we should pray, but it is better not to walk into danger when you don't have to. *Never mind, I'm on my way*, she thought. *I just hope that I'll be okay.* She knew that by praying, her grandfather could not save her, but because of his prayers, she could be saved by God.

It was as if the sun was long instead

of round, according to the long rays that extended about one-half of a mile on the railroad route. Then a curve and a cluster of trees kept the rest of the railroad from view. Brenda came walking fast to the part where a large pipe was under the track to cause the water to flow away from the railway.

While coming between the two railings near the pipe, Brenda began to jog, since a half mile of walking had not taken her as far as she would like to have been by now. With a tissue she wiped the sweat that seeped from her curly hair. The 90-degree weather was causing her arm to become red. Wearing pants brought some comfort from the piercing sun.

Suddenly, boys came from below the bank. They crept toward her from all sides—moving in back of her and in front until they were in a circle around her. They sneered and grinned at her. Their look was that of a triumphant person after a wild horse had been restrained.

Brenda's egotistic drive slipped away, although she continued at a crawling pace. Her reddened face and enlarged pupils scored insane fear! The glare from the sunlight was like a spinning wheel making her too dizzy to know one face from the other. Her pounding heart became weak. Robbery, rape, torture, all these thoughts crammed together in her head, making it impossible for her to relate to one particular thought. Trembling, she definitely stammered, "Oh, Ga, Ga, God—Grand, da, da, Daddy."

The teenagers' grins faded. A streak of humanity softened their cruel gaze. The upper part of their bodies fell back at the same time. It was as though they were being pushed against the chest by an invisible hand. To refuse to step back would mean they would fall down.

Brenda went through the opening that two of them presented when they moved from in front of her. She was weak from fear and was unable to run. Slowly she disappeared around the curve, taking a quick peek to see the boys chattering with their backs turned. The heat wave dazzled in their medium and dark brown hair. None of them had said anything or made physical contact, so they could not be prosecuted by law.

When she called her grandfather on the phone, it was to say that she was safely at home.

When she mentioned the fearful episode to him, she said, "Granddaddy, you prayed. You had a strong belief that God would hear you. And I was saved by an invisible hand. Thanks be to God."

"Behold, the Lord's hand is not shortened, that it cannot save; neither his ear heavy, that it cannot hear" (Isa. 59:1).

Then Satan Will Leave Us

The devil was being punished when Eve fell as his prey.
We've been beaten and stepped on for being that way.
We'll fast and pray (Mark 9:29)
and keep in touch with God's words.
Then Satan will leave us—leave us alone.
The dragon has teased me and marked me.
He even made me unkind.
I'll pray more and talk more to Jesus, my Lord.
Then Satan will leave us—leave us alone.
God's Spirit will help us to keep His commandments.
But we must watch what we do so that

God will accept (Matt. 13:43).
Then Satan will leave us—leave us alone.

We invite you to view the complete
selection of titles we publish at:

www.AspectBooks.com

Scan with your mobile
device to go directly
to our website.

Please write or email us your praises, reactions, or
thoughts about this or any other book we publish at:

P.O. Box 954
Ringgold, GA 30736

info@AspectBooks.com

Aspect Books titles may be purchased in bulk for
educational, business, fund-raising, or sales promotional use.
For information, please e-mail

BulkSales@AspectBooks.com

Finally, if you are interested in seeing
your own book in print, please contact us at

publishing@AspectBooks.com

We would be happy to review your manuscript for free.

www.ingramcontent.com/pod-product-compliance
Lightning Source LLC
Chambersburg PA
CBHW070544170426
43200CB00011B/2543